I don't pray in order to make life work;

I make life work so that I can pray.

_____

Praying always with all prayer and supplication in the Spirit.

Ephesians 6:18

The greatest honor in David's life was not being king of Israel or the writer of many psalms; it was being quoted three times on the cross.

What kind of journey would you have to walk in order to write the kind of thing Jesus would *want* to quote on the cross?

"My God, my God, why have You forsaken Me?" Matthew 27:46
"I thirst!" John 19:28
"Father, 'into Your hands I commit My spirit.'" Luke 23:46

If you're not distracted by Him,

you're not seeing Him.

_____

Yes, he is altogether lovely.

Song 5:16

You were never intended to carry your god;

you were intended to be carried by your God.

"They have no knowledge, who carry the wood of their carved image,

and pray to a god that cannot save."

Isaiah 45:20

"Even to your old age, I am He, and even to gray hairs I will carry you!

I have made, and I will bear; even I will carry, and will deliver you."

Isaiah 46:4

How could it possibly be said that the cross was
God's gentleness with Jesus?

When you look at the depravity of man and
the glory to which Christ has lifted him,
the cross was God's most gentle way to accomplish that.

Similarly, when you see the heights to
which God has lifted you, you will finally
realize your journey was gentle.

———————————

Your gentleness has made me great.

Psalm 18:35

We're fighting for a crown, not in order to wear it

but to have something to cast down.

God dignifies us with sonship, glory, exploits, and honor that

we might enjoy the great privilege of casting it all at His feet.

———————————————

The twenty-four elders fall down before Him who sits on the throne

and worship Him who lives forever and ever, and cast their

crowns before the throne.

Revelation 4:10

You can't be sent *from* God unless you're first *with* God.

———————————————

There was a man sent from God, whose name was John.

John 1:6

Satan was more bloodied by the cross than Jesus Christ.

Though your trial might mean you take it in the heel,

your obedience means your adversary takes it in the head.

———————————————————

"And I will put enmity between you and the woman, and between your seed and her

Seed; He shall bruise your head, and you shall bruise His heel."

Genesis 3:15

God will take a daunting, depressing mountain and level it into a fruitful plain to feed a generation from His goodness to you.

If ever a morbid mountain was turned into a fruitful plain that has fed an entire planet, it was the desolate mountain of Calvary!

How will your gloomy mountain be turned into a fruitful plain? "Not by might nor by power, but by My Spirit."

So he answered and said to me: "This is the word of the LORD to Zerubbabel: 'Not by might nor by power, but by My Spirit,' says the LORD of hosts. "Who are you, O great mountain? Before Zerubbabel you shall become a plain! And he shall bring forth the capstone with shouts of 'Grace, grace to it!"'"
Zechariah 4:6-7

The cross is the only thing God intended to do singlehandedly.

Since then, He does everything in partnership with us.

We then, as workers together with Him also plead with you not to receive

the grace of God in vain.

2 Corinthians 6:1

Jesus' primary concern is not for our comfort or
self-actualization; He's looking for us to be fruitful.

Every branch in Me that does not bear fruit He takes away; and every branch
that bears fruit He prunes, that it may bear more fruit.

John 15:2

JANUARY 12

Unanswered prayers avail nothing.

Press all the way through to answer.

———————————————————

"Ask, and you will receive, that your joy may be full."

John 16:24

God births babies en masse, He makes disciples in small groups,

and He shapes fathers in solitude.

I write to you, little children, because your sins are forgiven you for His name's sake.

I write to you, fathers, because you have known Him who is from the beginning.

I write to you, young men, because you have overcome the wicked one.

1 John 2:12-13

The cross cries out, "Anything for love!"

The cross is the most articulate and passionate way to say,

"I love you."

"For God so loved the world that He gave."

John 3:16

Jesus' life illustrates this important kingdom principle:

You don't have to sin in order to learn.

———————————————————

Though He was a Son, yet He learned obedience by the things which He suffered.

Hebrews 5:8

We are to please God and persuade men—not

(as we are too often inclined) to persuade God and please men.

———————————————————

For do I now persuade men, or God? Or do I seek to please men?

For if I still pleased men, I would not be a bondservant of Christ.

Galatians 1:10

He who waits for God's morning waits in total confidence.

Morning's advent is guaranteed, unstoppable.

God will come to you!

My soul waits for the Lord more than those who watch for the morning—

yes, more than those who watch for the morning.

Psalm 130:6

Love is perfected when we no longer fear God's fiery dealings,

but welcome the severe mercy that redirects our lives.

There is no fear in love; but perfect love casts out fear, because fear

involves torment. But he who fears has not been made perfect in love.

1 John 4:18

Jesus didn't die on the cross to gain a Bride who

yawns in His face on Sunday morning.

Jesus died to gain for Himself a Bride who has fire in her eyes

for Him like He has fire in His eyes for her.

His eyes like a flame of fire.

Revelation 1:14

Jesus didn't endure the cross in order to give us

90 hot minutes once a week on Sunday morning.

He died to give us a burning, fiery, intimate,

24/7 love relationship with Him.

You can't pass your accomplishments or giftings or attainments to another generation. Those things might impress, but they don't inspire.

The only thing universally transferable to the next generation is a life of prayer.

That's because a life of prayer is available to all regardless of privilege, economic status, education, or intelligence.

JANUARY 22

I resolve to have more faith in God's faithfulness to fulfill His word

than in the weakness of my flesh to fall short of His promises.

_____

For it is God who works in you both to will and to do for His good pleasure.

Philippians 2:13

Just because you're in a long, dusty wilderness does

not necessarily mean you are weak in faith.

It was *because* of their faith that Caleb and Joshua

found themselves in a 40-year trek through the wilderness.

A fire goes before God. So if you're feeling the fire of God in

your life, take heart—it means He is coming to you.

A fire goes before Him, and burns up His enemies round about.

Psalm 97:3

There are two ways we receive from God. Some things are *given*

to us, and some things are *bought*.

We love the things freely

given us by God, but to get the most valuable things

in the kingdom we'll have to pay a price.

"It is your Father's good pleasure to give you the kingdom."

Luke 12:32

"I counsel you to buy from Me gold refined in the fire, that you may be rich."

Revelation 3:18

When the time of testing comes and the fire is turned up in your life,

you have a choice: Give up, or go for the gold.

"I counsel you to buy from Me gold refined in the fire, that you may be rich."

Revelation 3:18

Sometimes God breaks off the purposes of your heart

so that He can bring you into His.

My purposes are broken off.

Job 17:11

Solomon got the promotion without the pruning and self-destructed.

David and Joseph got the pruning first and were preserved.

God loves you too much to give you the promotion without the pruning.

God is a consuming fire. Get into the presence of God and

you may get more than you bargained for.

———————————————————————

For the LORD your God is a consuming fire, a jealous God.

Deuteronomy 4:24

Jesus walks on water. To follow Him,

you've got to walk on water, too.

And Peter answered Him and said, "Lord, if it is You, command me

to come to You on the water."

Matthew 14:28

Your trial has so changed you that time spent with Jesus is no longer

a regimen or discipline; it has become a matter of sheer survival.

———————————

"Man shall not live by bread alone, but by every word that proceeds

from the mouth of God."

Matthew 4:4

A common symptom of spiritual pride is

sincere decision-making without consulting God.

When uncertain, wait.

Faith makes no frantic decisions in the face of crisis.

Faith waits upon God until the path to take becomes clear.

––––––––––––––––

"Whoever believes will not act hastily."

Isaiah 28:16

FEBRUARY 3

It's sobering to consider that we can have

our prayer answered but be impoverished for it.

———————————————

And He gave them their request, but sent leanness into their soul.

Psalm 106:15

There is no hotter flame than waiting on God.

Lead me in Your truth and teach me, for You are

the God of my salvation; on You I wait all the day.

Psalm 25:5

FEBRUARY 5

You can draw still closer to God.

Don't settle for the intimacy with God you now have.

———————————

Draw near to God and He will draw near to you.

James 4:8

Fast answers produce shallow benefits.

Fast answers don't change us.

Sometimes God delays the answer to our prayers

in order to transform us into the image of Christ.

He wants us to emerge from our trial both healed *and* changed.

FEBRUARY 7

May the Holy Spirit give you deep ownership of the reality that

you are wildly and irrevocably loved and enjoyed by God!

───────────────────────

"I in them, and You in Me; that they may be made perfect in one,

and that the world may know that You have sent Me,

and have loved them as You have loved Me."

John 17:23

If you resolve to live a life of prayer, it will be both the glory

of your life and the thing for which men will reproach you.

People will despise your values, but in heaven's eyes

the glory of your values will be a memorial.

How long, O you sons of men, will you turn my glory to shame?

Psalm 4:2

FEBRUARY 9

Many people are frustrated because they adopted a vision

that required others to line up with the vision.

But people never line up.

Instead, make the knowledge of Christ the great quest of your life,

and then nobody can hinder your pursuit.

They may be able to hinder your function in the body of Christ,

but they can't stop your secret life in God.

The grace of Jesus has granted to the believer

the great privilege of "burning before the throne."

And from the throne proceeded lightnings, thunderings, and voices.

Seven lamps of fire were burning before the throne,

which are the seven Spirits of God.

Revelation 4:5

FEBRUARY 11

You're going to burn for all eternity. The only question is where.

The Holy Spirit took over our tongues at Pentecost to convey,

"I want your tongue on fire, not from hell but from heaven."

_____

And the tongue is a fire, a world of iniquity.

The tongue is so set among our members that it defiles the whole body,

and sets on fire the course of nature; and it is set on fire by hell.

James 3:6

A god is anything to which we ascribe the power to deliver us.

What has that power in your life?

_____

And the rest of it he makes into a god, his carved image.

He falls down before it and worships it, prays to it and says,

"Deliver me, for you are my god!"

Isaiah 44:17

Any god that cannot deliver you does not deserve your worship.

"Your God, whom you serve continually, He will deliver you."

Daniel 6:16

FEBRUARY 15

The more sublime your goal, the more help you need.

———————————————

"I will strengthen you, yes, I will help you."

Isaiah 41:10

Prayer is the immune system of the body of Christ.

And the prayer of faith will save the sick, and the Lord will raise him up.

And if he has committed sins, he will be forgiven.

James 5:15

Intercession is a response to pain.

Intercession is the response of the heart

that is grieved over the human condition.

Leprosy is a disease that removes feeling from body members.

Prayerlessness is spiritual leprosy, for it indicates insensibility.

There's trouble in the body, but we're feeling no pain.

FEBRUARY 19

Sin is like a cancer; God's glory is like radiation on that cancer.

Get in His presence and stay there!

But we all, with unveiled face, beholding as in a mirror the glory of the Lord,

are being transformed into the same image from glory to glory,

just as by the Spirit of the Lord.

2 Corinthians 3:18

When circumstances or emotions are successful at robbing

your secret place, don't get guilty—get indignant!

FEBRUARY 21

The secret place was Jesus' "womb of the morning," the place where

life incubated, where creativity and power percolated.

Intimate communion with God is the womb from

which human history is changed.

_____

Your people shall be volunteers in the day of Your power; in the beauties of holiness,

from the womb of the morning, You have the dew of Your youth.

Psalm 110:3

The foremost indicator of the spiritual health of a church community is the level of spiritual hunger among the believers.

Said another way, healthy saints have a voracious appetite for the word and the Spirit.

We tend to view ourselves according to the flesh and end up

despising the very deposit of God in our lives.

Decide right now to regard yourself no longer according to the flesh.

Do not despise or minimize the Holy Spirit anointing on your life.

Therefore, from now on, we regard no one according to the flesh.

2 Corinthians 5:16

We want the anointing of Jesus—the kind of anointing

that comes upon and remains upon our lives.

If you have a Dove on your shoulder, and you want Him

to stay there, then how must you walk?

_____

And John bore witness, saying, "I saw the Spirit descending

from heaven like a dove, and He remained upon Him."

John 1:32

Long wait, deep work.

Once you're on the other side of your trial,

you'll realize that the duration of your crucible was strategic.

———————————————————

Knowing that the testing of your faith produces patience.

But let patience have its perfect work, that you may be

perfect and complete, lacking nothing.

James 1:3-4

Deprivation produces desire.

Famine makes us hungry.

Drought makes us thirsty.

"Blessed are those who hunger and thirst for righteousness,

for they shall be filled."

Matthew 5:6

FEBRUARY 27

Two sicknesses from which you never want a total cure:

Lovesickness longs to see Christ's face.

Heartsickness longs for the manifest power of Christ's hand.

———————————————

"Sustain me with cakes of raisins,

refresh me with apples, for I am lovesick."

Song of Solomon 2:5

Hope deferred makes the heart sick,

but when the desire comes, it is a tree of life.

Proverbs 13:12

Once you've discovered happy holiness, you realize that

nothing is worth losing this kind of nearness to God.

———————————————

Worship the LORD in the beauty of holiness.

Psalm 29:2

I get all of God and He gets all of me.

That exchange definitely inured to my benefit!

"I am my beloved's, and my beloved is mine. He feeds his flock among the lilies."

Song of Solomon 6:3

There is a kind of compassion, satanically inspired,

that seeks to save people from their cross.

———————————————

And He began to teach them that the Son of Man must suffer many things,

and be rejected by the elders and chief priests and scribes, and be killed,

and after three days rise again. He spoke this word openly.

Then Peter took Him aside and began to rebuke Him.

Mark 8:31-32

If God crucifies you, take it personally.

If God resurrects you, take it personally.

My God, My God, why have You forsaken Me?

Psalm 22:1

In crucifixion, God makes the whole thing personal for you.

In resurrection, He demonstrates that

the whole thing is personal to Him.

Your crucifixion and burial will happen without a fight.

Hell will even help it happen.

The warfare isn't over crucifixion but resurrection.

Having disarmed principalities and powers, He made

a public spectacle of them, triumphing over them in it.

Colossians 2:15

You can get a measure of help or relief from human sources.

But if it's salvation you want, Jesus is the only source.

———————————————

Nor is there salvation in any other, for there is no other name under heaven

given among men by which we must be saved.

Acts 4:12

A lesson to be learned from the godly king, Josiah:

Don't go into a war God's not calling you to.

---

*After all this, when Josiah had prepared the temple, Necho king of Egypt came up
to fight against Carchemish by the Euphrates; and Josiah went out against him.
But he sent messengers to him, saying, "What have I to do with you, king of Judah?
I have not come against you this day, but against the house with which I have war;
for God commanded me to make haste. Refrain from meddling with God, who is
with me, lest He destroy you." Nevertheless Josiah would not turn his face from him,
but disguised himself so that he might fight with him, and did not heed the words of
Necho from the mouth of God. So he came to fight in the Valley of Megiddo. And the
archers shot King Josiah; and the king said to his servants, "Take me away,
for I am severely wounded." His servants therefore took him out of that chariot
and put him in the second chariot that he had, and they brought him to Jerusalem.
So he died, and was buried in one of the tombs of his fathers.
And all Judah and Jerusalem mourned for Josiah.
2 Chronicles 35:20-24*

Those who shrink back from a God-ordained battle

could forfeit their destiny.

The children of Ephraim, being armed and carrying bows, turned back in the

day of battle. They did not keep the covenant of God; they refused to

walk in His law, and forgot His works and His wonders that He had shown them...

Moreover He rejected the tent of Joseph, and did not choose the tribe of Ephraim...

Psalm 78:9-11, 67

To do the quickest work, God waits.

God puts your life on hold in order to accelerate your growth curve.

The heat and pressure of waiting on God produces

a maturity beyond your years.

————————————————————

Until the time that his word came to pass, the word of the LORD tested him.

The king sent and released him...to bind his princes at his pleasure,

and teach his elders wisdom.

Psalm 105:19-22

When you know your supernatural ministry will get you crucified,

you're not as eager as others to see it launched.

———————————————

Jesus said to her, "Woman, what does your concern have to do with Me?

My hour has not yet come." His mother said to the servants,

"Whatever He says to you, do it."

John 2:4-5

At the cross, Jesus prayed like a Lion and died like a Lamb.

"Behold, the Lion of the tribe of Judah"...And I looked, and behold,

in the midst of the throne and of the four living creatures,

and in the midst of the elders, stood a Lamb as though it had been slain.

Revelation 5:5-6

If you want to see what's inside a man, impale him to a cross. What came out of Jesus: forgiveness, promise, loyalty, and faith.

———————————————————

"Father, forgive them, for they do not know what they do." Luke 23:34

"Assuredly, I say to you, today you will be with Me in Paradise." Luke 23:43

"My God, My God, why have You forsaken Me?" Matthew 27:46

"It is finished!" John 19:30

Why does God allow so many trials and strange twists in your journey?

Because you can't get a great story out of a boring plot.

You number my wanderings; put my tears into Your bottle;

are they not in Your book?

Psalm 56:8

Refuse intimidation!

David had to shake off the intimidation of his brother (1 Samuel 17:28),

his boss (1 Samuel 17:38), and his enemy (1 Samuel 17:44).

———————————————

And David said, "What have I done now? Is there not a cause?"

1 Samuel 17:29

When you know the power of God, you know that all

you need from God is the tiniest crumb.

"You do not know...the power of God"

Mark 12:24

And she answered and said to Him, "Yes, Lord, yet even the little dogs

under the table eat from the children's crumbs."

Mark 7:28

Holiness keeps you on the road to your promises.

A highway shall be there, and a road, and it shall be called

the Highway of Holiness.

Isaiah 35:8

Don't look at the powers of darkness to learn spiritual warfare.

The cross proved their lack of competence.

Look at your Champion!

_____

To the intent that now the manifold wisdom of God might be made known

by the church to the principalities and powers in the heavenly places.

Ephesians 3:10

David bested Goliath with a stick and five stones.

Jesus bested Satan with a stick and five wounds.

Neither used the weapons of his opponent.

So the Philistine said to David, "Am I a dog that you come to me with sticks?"

1 Samuel 17:43

MARCH 19

You can mount up with wings only if the wind blows.

Wait on God and one day the Spirit's wind will blow.

———————————————————

But those who wait on the LORD...shall mount up with wings like eagles.
Isaiah 40:31

Sometimes the best kingdom decisions don't make sense to

those who are guided by Profit/Loss Reports.

Ephraim is oppressed and broken in judgment,

because he willingly walked by human precept.

Hosea 5:11

Fear is agreement with the devil.

Faith is agreement with God.

"All things are possible to him who believes."

Mark 9:23

I'm not looking ahead to a time when I *will* be healed;

I'm looking back to the time I *was* healed.

Who Himself bore our sins in His own body on the tree, that we, having died to sins, might live for righteousness—by whose stripes you were healed.

1 Peter 2:24

Resurrection is God's way of saying, "I'm collecting on

everything I've invested in you through your suffering."

God labors meticulously to refine you into a useful vessel.

He would never cast you away after investing

so much into your preparation.

_____

Take away the dross from silver, and it will go to the silversmith for jewelry.

Proverbs 25:4

Fear lest you come short of inhabiting the promises

God intends for you to possess.

Therefore, since a promise remains of entering His rest,

let us fear lest any of you seem to have come short of it.

Hebrews 4:1

Guard vigilantly against the common temptation to think

excessively or disparagingly of yourself.

Have faith to view yourself in sound judgment.

———————————————————

For I say, through the grace given to me, to everyone who is among you,

not to think of himself more highly than he ought to think, but

to think soberly, as God has dealt to each one a measure of faith.

Romans 12:3

Unbelief is foolish and beastly.

It is a wild, untamed, unruly beast in the soul. Be rid of it!

I was so foolish and ignorant; I was like a beast before You.

Psalm 73:22

You should lay hands on the sick and raise them up because,

if you were the sick one, you'd want someone to do that to you.

"Therefore, whatever you want men to do to you,

do also to them, for this is the Law and the Prophets."

Matthew 7:12

For years I labored to become a better leader;

now I labor to become a better follower.

Fervent followers of Jesus make the best leaders.

———————————————

Then He said to them, "Follow Me, and I will make you fishers of men."

Matthew 4:19

Take down a cop wearing a badge,

and you'll have the entire force after you.

Similarly, if Satan hits one of Christ's soldiers,

all of heaven's armies take it personally.

MARCH 31

Christ's resurrection was quiet on earth but loud in hell.

Seek to make an impact in the spiritual, not the natural, realm.

God didn't allow Joshua to incorporate the war machinery

of his vanquished enemies into his military arsenal.

Why do we sometimes pick up the very devices that didn't

protect the ungodly, and use them to try to protect ourselves?

So Joshua did to them as the LORD had told him:

he hamstrung their horses and burned their chariots with fire.

Joshua 11:9

He looks with favor upon the upright. To put it another way—

if He likes you, He looks at you.

_____

The eyes of the LORD are on the righteous, and His ears are open to their cry.

Psalm 34:15

We surrender to the nails that curtail our freedoms

and restrict our options.

———————————————

I have been crucified with Christ.

Galatians 2:20

APRIL 4

The Sabbath is to the week what the secret place is to the day.

———————————————————

"Six days shall work be done, but the seventh day is a Sabbath

of solemn rest, a holy convocation. You shall do no work on it;

it is the Sabbath of the LORD in all your dwellings."

Leviticus 23:3

You've wondered, "Why are Your corrections more forceful

in my life than in the lives of my peers?"

His answer: "It's not that you have uncommon issues,

but you are called to an uncommon anointing."

_____

He has not dealt with us according to our sins.

Psalm 103:10

To the degree I am concerned about my appearance before men,

to that degree I lack concern for my appearance before God.

To the degree I am touched by the fear of man I lack the fear of God.

The smartest creatures in the created order—the seraphim—

just stand and stare at God. It's the smartest thing you could ever do.

And in the midst of the throne, and around the throne,

were four living creatures full of eyes in front and in back.

Revelation 4:6

The more time you spend in the *logos* (written word),

the greater your chances of receiving a *rhema* (spoken word).

───────────────────

"'Man shall not live by bread alone, but by every word [rhema]

that proceeds from the mouth of God.'"

Matthew 4:4

The reproach of the cross becomes the backdrop against which the glory of the resurrection sparkles as a glistening jewel.

Similarly, the reproach of your trial becomes the backdrop against which the glory of your deliverance shines in dazzling brilliance. Therefore, despise the reproach.

Looking unto Jesus, the author and finisher of our faith, who for the joy that was set before Him endured the cross, despising the shame.

Hebrews 12:2

We are shrewd but not fearful. We are fearless but not careless.

"But beware of men, for they will deliver you up to

councils and scourge you in their synagogues."

Matthew 10:17

"Therefore do not fear them. For there is nothing covered that will not be revealed,

and hidden that will not be known."

Matthew 10:26

The fear of the Lord is a jewel with which God rewards the righteous.

You cannot have too much of this treasure. Get all you can!

———————————

The fear of the LORD is His treasure.

Isaiah 33:6

Can I believe in a way that makes all things possible?

Yes, I can have mountain-moving faith. I can have faith for anything—but only as Christ strengthens me.

Jesus said to him, "If you can believe,

all things are possible to him who believes."

Mark 9:23

I can do all things through Christ who strengthens me.

Philippians 4:13

Mourn the undesirable things within you that you yourself cannot change. Then God will comfort you by changing you.

————————————

"Blessed are those who mourn, for they shall be comforted."

Matthew 5:4

Psalm 14:1 calls unbelief foolishness.

There is nothing more foolish than not to believe the word of God.

"O foolish ones, and slow of heart to believe in all

that the prophets have spoken!"

Luke 24:25

Unbelief, with its logic, can appear so wise but actually is very foolish.

Faith can appear foolish but is, in fact, utterly wise.

Has not God made foolish the wisdom of this world? For since,

in the wisdom of God, the world through wisdom did not know God,

it pleased God through the foolishness of the message

preached to save those who believe.

1 Corinthians 1:20-21

Jesus was born naked and He died naked.

Job actually prophesied Christ's crucifixion.

———————————————————

"Naked I came from my mother's womb, and naked shall I return there."

Job 1:21

Healed just days before Christ's crucifixion, Bartimaeus was

most likely at Calvary. Consider what that spectacle

must have looked like to his just-opened eyes.

_____

Immediately he received his sight and followed Jesus on the road.

Mark 10:52

One of the most gripping statements in the Old Testament on Calvary:

"For the redemption of their souls is costly" (Psalm 49:8).

Jesus distinguished between trials and suffering.
He characterized His three years of ministry
as "trials" but He had yet to suffer.

Those who have merely known trials cannot fully
empathize with those who have truly suffered.

"But you are those who have continued with Me in My trials."

Luke 22:28

"With fervent desire I have desired to eat this Passover

with you before I suffer."

Luke 22:15

Behold the resurrection!

When you can't comprehend it, just behold it.

"I am He who lives, and was dead, and behold, I am alive forevermore. Amen."

Revelation 1:18

All that resurrection requires is deadness.

With God, there is no such thing as "too dead."

It's never too late for resurrection.

"I am the resurrection and the life. He who believes in Me,

though he may die, he shall live."

John 11:25

Jesus didn't do funerals. Weddings yes, funerals no.

The one funeral He did attend He "ruined" by raising the widow's son.

———————————————————

Then He came and touched the open coffin, and those who carried him stood still.

And He said, "Young man, I say to you, arise."

Luke 7:14

Each crown Jesus wears represents a specific conquest.

He has "many crowns" because He's never lost a war.

It bodes ill for the one against whom this undefeated

Champion "makes war."

_____

Now I saw heaven opened, and behold, a white horse. And He who sat on him

was called Faithful and True, and in righteousness He judges and makes war.

His eyes were like a flame of fire, and on His head were many crowns.

Rev. 19:11-12

APRIL 24

Jesus created the human body for crucifixion. He put all those

nerve endings in the hands and feet because He wanted to

feel our sorrows.

He feels as intensely about you as His cross was painful.

A Man of sorrows and acquainted with grief.

Isaiah 53:3

Israel's biggest problem is not Islam nor the Palestinians

nor Iran, but God. She is in rebellion to a covenant

from which God will not relent.

"What you have in your mind shall never be, when you say, 'We will be like the Gentiles,

like the families in other countries, serving wood and stone.'"

Ezekiel 20:32

When God performed wonders, the Israelites saw miracles,

but Moses saw God.

He made known His ways to Moses, His acts to the children of Israel.

Psalm 103:7

When God gives you justice, it will not happen quietly in a corner

but will shine forth as the noonday, evident to all.

———————————————————

He shall bring forth your righteousness as the light,

and your justice as the noonday.

Psalm 37:6

Don't try to be someone else.

We need you to be you!

———————————————————

"Every part [of the body] does its share."

Ephesians 4:16

Unbelief is something akin to a spiritual learning disability.

The slow of heart are spiritually underdeveloped.

Lord, make us swift to believe!

"O foolish ones, and slow of heart *to believe in all that*

the prophets have spoken!"

Luke 24:25

APRIL 30

Never assume that the silence of God means

He approves of your course of action.

———————————————————

These things you have done, and I kept silent;

you thought that I was altogether like you; but I will rebuke you,

and set them in order before your eyes.

Psalm 50:21

If you mobilize the children without the hearts of the fathers turned to them, you don't have a youth movement but a rebellion.

———————————————

"He will also go before Him in the spirit and power of Elijah,
'to turn the hearts of the fathers to the children' and the disobedient
to the wisdom of the just, to make ready a people prepared for the Lord."

Luke 1:17

For three years everyone just stared at Jesus.

They scrutinized and studied His every expression, move, and word.

He was—and is—utterly amazing to behold!

———————————————

That which we have seen with our eyes, which we have looked upon.

1 John 1:1

The cross is the wood on the altar of my heart that

keeps my fervency alive and fiery.

_____

Where there is no wood, the fire goes out.
Proverbs 26:20

The cross is the balance beam of Christianity.

Any doctrinal emphasis that strays from the centrality of the cross becomes imbalanced.

For I determined not to know anything among you

except Jesus Christ and Him crucified.

1 Corinthians 2:2

If you can't get it through the cross, it doesn't fit in the kingdom.

There are only two spirits at work in the earth. Ever.

The one seeks only to glorify God; the other labors only to kill Him.

Which spirit has your allegiance?

_____

And I saw the beast, the kings of the earth, and their armies,

gathered together to make war against Him who sat

on the horse and against His army.

Revelation 19:19

Faith supersedes understanding. There are some things about

God you'll never understand until you first believe them to be true.

By faith we understand that the worlds were framed by the word of God.

Hebrews 11:3

Enduring and coping are worlds apart.

The world *copes* because they expect no change.

Believers *endure* because they hold to promise.

For you have need of endurance, so that after you have done

the will of God, you may receive the promise.

Hebrews 10:36

Coping seeks relief; endurance seeks salvation.

Coping accepts the circumstances as one's new home;

endurance is always a sojourner.

Be a boat not a wave.

Hoist a sail. Capture the power of your storm

to press into the face of Christ.

A sailboat harnesses

the power of contrary winds to forge forward

into the very winds that resist its progress.

_____

But let him ask in faith, with no doubting, for he who doubts is

like a wave of the sea driven and tossed by the wind.

James 1:6

Jesus responds in gentleness to issues that we think are

alarming and necessitate strict correction,

e.g. envy among the disciples (Mark 10:41-45).

Jesus responds in vehemence to issues that don't alarm us at all,

e.g. the cleansing of the temple (John 2:14-17).

He is altogether unlike us.

Everybody tarries differently. Sit, kneel, cry, shout, or sleep.

No matter how you tarry, just be there when Holy Spirit shows up.

"Behold, I send the Promise of My Father upon you;

but tarry in the city of Jerusalem until you are endued

with power from on high."

Luke 24:49

Intimacy without power can never fully satisfy

because it is a non-reciprocal relationship.

I am my beloved's, and my beloved is mine.

Song of Solomon 6:3

Jacob had such ownership and confidence in his relationship
with God that he called Him after his own name:
"the Mighty God of Jacob."

Insert your own name in the blank, and talk
to your children about "the Mighty God of _____."

_____

"The arms of his hands were made strong by the

hands of the Mighty God of Jacob."

Genesis 49:24

The work of the cross was so massive, it took all

three Persons of the Trinity to pull it off.

The Father couldn't have done it without the Son's willingness

to offer Himself. The Son couldn't have done it without

the Holy Spirit empowering Him to drink the bitter cup

to the bottom. The Spirit couldn't have done it without

the Father's approval and orchestration.

There are no shortcuts to a great testimony.

Someone once said, "You just see the glory,

but you don't know the story."

Any temptation to envy someone else's glory

dissolves when you hear the agony of their story.

To the question, "Should I go to a doctor for this?"

my answer is, do whatever keeps you in faith.

_____

For whatever is not from faith is sin.

Romans 14:23

Don't despise the means God uses to make you desperate for Him.

Sometimes a prophet has to be wounded
before he can deliver his message.

If being God's messenger means being
wounded first, are you still in?

_____

Now a certain man of the sons of the prophets said to his neighbor by the
word of the LORD, "Strike me, please." And the man refused to strike him.
Then he said to him, "Because you have not obeyed the voice of the LORD,
surely, as soon as you depart from me, a lion shall kill you." And as soon as
he left him, a lion found him and killed him. And he found another man, and said,
"Strike me, please." So the man struck him, inflicting a wound. 1 Kings 20:35-37

Imagine such abundant gratefulness for what God has done for you that it interrupts and disturbs your sleep patterns!

At midnight I will rise to give thanks to You, because of Your righteous judgments.

Psalm 119:62

The glory of corporate worship is the dynamic in the midst of the saints

that cannot be experienced fully by those who catch the webcast.

We need worship services that leave people saying,

"You had to be there."

Burns cause scarring and desensitization.

You've not been burned by this fiery trial;

you're more sensitive than ever to the things of God.

When you walk through the fire, you shall not be burned,

nor shall the flame scorch you.

Isaiah 43:2

It's the pure in heart who see God.

Then, when they do, they call themselves vile.

_____

Blessed are the pure in heart, for they shall see God.

Matthew 5:8

"Behold, I am vile...I have heard of You by the hearing of the ear,

but now my eye sees You."

Job 40:4; 42:5

MAY 24

Job represents the man who has an experience

at the hand of God for which he has no theology.

Don't boast in what you have (which is all things); boast in who has you.

_____

Whether Paul or Apollos or Cephas, or the world or life or death,

or things present or things to come—all are yours. And you are Christ's.

1 Corinthians 3:22-23

Jesus called the Holy Spirit the Helper. He's all the help I need.

If I can't get it from Him, I don't need it.

"But the Helper, the Holy Spirit...will teach you all things."

John 14:26

A slave's welfare is the responsibility of his master.

A master would be insulted if his slave went to someone other

than him for help—as though he were not able to care for his own.

Paul, a bondservant of Jesus Christ.

Romans 1:1

MAY 28

I am thrice made by God.

1. He created me.

2. He made me a new creation in Christ.

3. And He is making me into Christ's image.

———————————————

For whom He foreknew, He also predestined to be conformed to the image of His Son.

Romans 8:29

Want to grow in faith and love? Then cling to Jesus

because faith and love are to be found only in Him.

And the grace of our Lord was exceedingly abundant,

with faith and love which are in Christ Jesus.

1 Timothy 1:14

"A woman can do with her body what she wants," they say.

But a fetus has a distinct DNA.

It's the body of another. Abortion is murder.

———————————————

For You formed my inward parts; You covered me in my mother's womb.

Psalm 139:13

I long for the kind of faith that causes Jesus to marvel.

"For I also am a man placed under authority, having soldiers under me.

And I say to one, 'Go,' and he goes; and to another, 'Come,' and he comes;

and to my servant, 'Do this,' and he does it." When Jesus heard these things,

He marveled at him, *and turned around and said to the crowd that followed Him,*

"I say to you, I have not found such great faith, not even in Israel!"

Luke 7:8-9

Lengthy trials have the potential to produce in you

the kind of faith that not only triggers your release,

but the release of others as well.

I used to think the blood of Jesus was only for certain limited uses.

But Hebrews 13:20-21 takes the lid off that,

revealing that the blood enables us for "every good work."

Now I realize I can plead the blood over most everything!

Now may the God of peace who brought up our Lord Jesus from the dead,

that great Shepherd of the sheep, through the blood of the everlasting

covenant, make you complete in every good work to do His will.

Hebrews 13:20-21

Use temporal things for eternal advantage.

Said another way, use what you've got for where you're going.

"And I say to you, make friends for yourselves by unrighteous mammon, that when you fail, they may receive you into an everlasting home."

Luke 16:9

You cannot have authority over unclean spirits as long as

anything unclean has a home within you.

For He said to him, "Come out of the man, unclean spirit!"

Mark 5:8

What someone is willing to pay for something determines its value.

Calvary's price reveals how much God values you.

Struggling to find joy right now? Don't forget,

Jesus is rejoicing exuberantly over your life today.

Rejoice with Him!

Rejoice with those who rejoice.

Romans 12:15

I can have a successful ministry

(in terms of impact, numbers, profile)

and be unsuccessful in my call to know Jesus.

That I may know Him.

Philippians 3:10

Faith is our first and highest response to the hearing of the word.

Lend the full weight of your entire being to believing His word!

So then faith comes by hearing, and hearing by the word of God.

Romans 10:17

You don't obey your way into faith; you believe your way into obedience.

The Pharisees proved that strict adherence to Scripture does not by itself produce faith in the human spirit.

"Woe to you, scribes and Pharisees, hypocrites! For you pay tithe of mint and anise and cumin, and have neglected the weightier matters of the law: justice and mercy and faith. These you ought to have done, without leaving the others undone."

Matthew 23:23

The Jews were so focused on Christ's coming earthly kingdom

that they missed the glory of the kingdom within.

Gentile believers are often so focused on God's kingdom

within they lose sight of the glory of Christ's coming earthly kingdom.

———————————————

They shall speak of the glory of Your kingdom, and talk of Your power.

Psalm 145:11

Any voter who doesn't vote is advertising his

prayerlessness for his nation.

If you're invested in prayer for your country, you'll vote.

Jesus said that healing someone was a good work.

May your life be replete with good works.

———————————————————

"Therefore it is lawful to do good on the Sabbath." Then He said to the man,

"Stretch out your hand." And he stretched it out,

and it was restored as whole as the other.

Matthew 12:12-13

JUNE 13

Proponents of "gay rights" appear compassionately merciful, but a

gay-approving society ultimately ends up being unmerciful.

Likewise also the men, leaving the natural use of the woman, burned in their

lust for one another, men with men committing what is shameful...being filled

with all unrighteousness, sexual immorality, wickedness, covetousness,

maliciousness...they are whisperers, backbiters, haters of God...unmerciful.

Romans 1:27-31

Jesus desired that nothing valuable be lost or wasted.

Many captives are wasting away in prisons of injustice.

Ask God for the spiritual authority to release captives,

so that nothing is lost.

———————————————

"Gather up the fragments that remain, so that nothing is lost."

John 6:12

JUNE 15

Beholding the extremity of Calvary gave Joseph of Arimathea

the courage to go public with his faith.

Beholding the cross always gives courage.

_____

Joseph of Arimathea, a prominent council member, who was himself waiting

for the kingdom of God, coming and taking courage, went in to Pilate and

asked for the body of Jesus.

Mark 15:43

Joseph of Arimathea and Nicodemus shared the singular privilege

of getting the actual shed blood of Jesus on themselves.

When you serve Jesus, you're getting stuff on you that

is more precious than you realize.

Joseph of Arimathea...asked Pilate that he might take away the body of Jesus;

and Pilate gave him permission...And Nicodemus, who at first came to Jesus

by night, also came...Then they took the body of Jesus.

John 19:38-40

Demonstrate your faith publicly before men and the

Lord will reward you with goodness in a public way.

Oh, how great is Your goodness...which You have prepared for those

who trust in You in the presence of the sons of men!

Psalm 31:19

The anointing changes the lens through which you see. In 1 Samuel 16:13, David came under an anointing that gave him a perspective like no one else in his generation.

Everyone else looked at Goliath and saw a champion; David saw an "uncircumcised Philistine." Everyone else looked at Israel's troops and saw an under-staffed band of losers; David saw "the armies of the living God."

"For who is this uncircumcised Philistine, that he should defy the armies of the living God?"

1 Samuel 17:26

The greatest paradoxes of the kingdom all surround the subject of faith.

Paradox denies us the luxury of putting God in a theological box.

One of the paradoxes of faith: We are pursuing things in God that can only be received as a gift from heaven.

How do I get the kingdom? Do I "take" the kingdom violently

or do I "receive" the kingdom meekly?

Jesus says, "Yes."

"And from the days of John the Baptist until now the kingdom of heaven

suffers violence, and the violent take it by force."

Matthew 11:12

"Assuredly, I say to you, whoever does not receive the kingdom of God

as a little child will by no means enter it."

Mark 10:15

Unbelief is faith in a lie.

Indeed, let God be true but every man a liar.

Romans 3:3

He who does not believe God has made Him a liar.

1 John 5:10

Unbelief is faith in what is.

_____

God...calls those things which do not exist as though they did.

Romans 4:17

While we do not look at the things which are seen,

but at the things which are not seen.

2 Corinthians 4:18

The Holy Spirit testifies that I am healed and whole. I agree with God.

By whose stripes you were healed.

1 Peter 2:24

You cannot see God and think small things about Him.

Now to Him who is able to do exceedingly abundantly above all that

we ask or think, according to the power that works in us.

Ephesians 3:20

Jesus gave us the command, "Give to everyone who asks of you"

(Luke 6:30) because He Himself lives by that precept.

He gives to everyone who asks of Him.

Be bold in prayer! Ask!

Jeremiah testified twice that God's people do not know His judgments.

Think about it. You don't know this side of God.

———————————————————

"Even the stork in the heavens knows her appointed times; and the turtledove,

the swift, and the swallow observe the time of their coming.

But My people do not know the judgment of the LORD."

Jeremiah 8:7

JUNE 27

Any society that establishes rules and laws, but then doesn't

enforce them, subjects its citizens to futility and anarchy.

Enforcement produces social order.

God is a masterful enforcer. He punishes those who violate His laws, and He rewards those who obey them.

God's judgments don't make Him abhorrent. To the contrary, it's the fact that God judges that makes His leadership so admirable and effective. This is why we exult in the judgments of God—we love the thoroughness of His leadership.

"Alleluia! Salvation and glory and honor and power belong to the Lord our God! For true and righteous are His judgments."

Revelation 19:1-2

Do not make the mistake of thinking God is incapable of evil.

God created hell, which is evil to those who experience it.

———————————————————

Show the things that are to come hereafter, that we may know that you are gods;

yes, do good or do evil, that we may be dismayed and see it together.

Isaiah 41:23

We live by every word that proceeds from God's mouth.

Even if it's a word of woe, it's still life to us.

———————————————

Is it not from the mouth of the Most High that woe and well-being proceed?

Lamentations 3:38

Satan caricaturizes child discipline as abusive and oppressive

in order to skew a generation against a God who disciplines.

———————————————————

My son, do not despise the chastening of the LORD...

For whom the LORD loves He corrects.

Proverbs 3:11-12

The means God uses to punish the disobedient and

refine the obedient are identical.

This is why those in a refining crucible feel such reproach.

The undiscerning assume them to be under divine punishment.

———————————————

For they persecute the ones You have struck, and talk of the grief

of those You have wounded.

Psalm 69:26

Crucifixion exposed not only Jesus but also everyone else around Him.

Your crucifixion exposes everyone around you, too.

"(Yes, a sword will pierce through your own soul also), that

the thoughts of many hearts may be revealed."

Luke 2:35

The Holy Spirit is deeply committed to restoring

the first commandment to first place in our lives.

He's making us into lovers who work rather than workers who love.

"'And you shall love the LORD your God with all your heart, with all your soul, with all your mind, and with all your strength.' This is the first commandment."

Mark 12:30

Peter and John weren't going to the prayer meeting to get the power to raise the lame—they already had it.

Most people, if they had the power to raise the lame, would blow off the prayer meeting. But prayer is so much more than just "getting powered up" for good works. It's about intimacy.

———————————————————————

Now Peter and John went up together to the temple at the hour of prayer... And a certain man lame from his mother's womb was...laid daily at the gate of the temple...who, seeing Peter and John about to go into the temple, asked for alms...And he took him by the right hand and lifted him up, and immediately his feet and ankle bones received strength. Acts 3:1-3, 7

When your flame of love for Jesus is pure, God can elevate
your light to serve the household of faith.

God places some ministries under a basket—that is,
He localizes their sphere. Why? Because the Lord is unwilling
to export the mixture in their flame, lest others emulate it.

———————————————————

*"Nor do they light a lamp and put it under a basket, but on a lampstand,
and it gives light to all who are in the house."*

Matthew 5:15

It's possible to do everything right and still experience

great distress and calamity.

Many are the afflictions of the righteous.

Psalm 34:19

It makes little difference to us whether we are on earth or in heaven.

Either way, we live every moment in intimacy with Jesus.

We're not waiting for eternity; we've already stepped into it.

When we cross over, little will change. We'll still be

about the exact same thing—living with Jesus.

———————————————————

Who died for us, that whether we wake or sleep, we should live together with Him.

1 Thessalonians 5:10

Moses, who spoke with God face to face,

was more humble than any other man on earth.

Seeing God humbles you because in seeing

Him you also see your own bankruptcy.

(Now the man Moses was very humble, more than all men who were on

the face of the earth)..."I speak with him face to face, even plainly,

and not in dark sayings; and he sees the form of the LORD."

Numbers 12:3, 8

The experience of one who boasts a great encounter with God but does not manifest a commensurate humility is questionable.

God only does wondrous, unforgettable things.

If it's boring, God didn't do it.

Blessed be the LORD God, the God of Israel,

who only does wondrous things!

Psalm 72:18

He has made His wonderful works to be remembered.

Psalm 111:4

Elders draft the battle plans;

princes (young leaders) lead the battle charge.

Elders channel the energy of the princes toward that which is effectual;

princes are the strong ones who get out there and push.

"Thus says the LORD: 'Have you seen all this great multitude? Behold, I will deliver it into your hand today, and you shall know that I am the LORD.'" So Ahab said, "By whom?" And he said, "Thus says the LORD: 'By the young leaders of the provinces.'" Then he said, "Who will set the battle in order?" And he answered, "You."

1 Kings 20:13-14

Old songs gather, new songs propel.

Worship leaders, use old (well-known) songs
to gather and galvanize a group of worshipers.

Use new songs to propel a community forward

into the fresh things of the Spirit.

Too many new songs can leave a group disengaged,

so come back to an old song and re-gather the room.

Worship leading is the artful employment of both old and new songs.

Terms of endearment the Lord has for you:

In Jeremiah 12:7 He calls you "the dearly beloved of My soul."

Isaiah 62:4 says, "The LORD delights in you."

You are "the yearning of [God's] heart" (Isaiah 63:15).

Jesus says, "You are all fair, my love" (Song of Solomon 4:7).

He calls you, "My dove, my perfect one...the only one"

(Song of Solomon 6:9).

At times Jesus reproached certain people.

Would you ever reproach others in a Christlike way,

or are you tempted to be "nicer" than Jesus?

_____

Then one of the lawyers answered and said to Him,

"Teacher, by saying these things You reproach us also."

Luke 11:45

That which is truly valuable or significant must be received from heaven.

If heaven won't give it, you don't want it.

"A man can receive nothing unless it has been given to him from heaven."

John 3:27

A new song is a response to something new God has done.

To sing a new song, you must have something fresh
from the Lord working in your heart.

———————————————

Let the word of Christ dwell in you richly in all wisdom, teaching and
admonishing one another in psalms and hymns and spiritual songs,
singing with grace in your hearts to the Lord.

Colossians 3:16

How can you speak evil of your brother,

but then affirm him when you're with him?

Speaking evil of your brother denies you the privilege

of encouraging him as you ought.

Do not speak evil of one another.

James 4:11

Therefore comfort each other and edify one another.

1 Thessalonians 5:11

Prison is a great equalizer.

Once you're in there, it matters little what got you there.

The same is true for hell.

"Have you also become as weak as we? Have you become like us?

Your pomp is brought down to Sheol."

Isaiah 14:10-11

I can claim that God's thoughts are precious to me,

but to what lengths will I go to receive them?

How precious also are Your thoughts to me, O God!

Psalm 139:17

Understanding into the person of Christ is the thing that

sets the heart on fire.

And they said to one another, "Did not our heart burn within us while

He talked with us on the road, and while He opened the Scriptures to us?"

Luke 24:32

Jesus is used to creatures who respond to Him with

the speed of lightning. Little wonder slowness of heart wearies Him.

———————————————————

The living creatures ran back and forth...like a flash of lightning.

Ezekiel 1:14

"O...slow of heart to believe."

Luke 24:25

Never view present smallness as defining future reach.

We are part of a kingdom that never stops growing.

Of the increase of His government and peace there will be no end.

Isaiah 9:7

The scribes should have feared Jesus for the authority He had with God; instead, they feared Him for the authority He had with men.

So really, it wasn't God they feared, but man.

The scribes and chief priests...feared Him,

because all the people were astonished at His teaching.

Mark 11:18

And they sought to lay hands on Him, but feared the multitude.

Mark 12:12

Fatherlessness can actually prepare for fatherhood. It was Joseph's fatherlessness in prison that prepared him to be a father to Pharaoh.

In prison, Joseph had to find God as his Father.

That's what made him a father to Pharaoh.

"So now it was not you who sent me here, but God; and He has made me a father to Pharaoh."

Genesis 45:8

Don't assume the fatherless will be dysfunctional parents

for lack of paternal influence.

Parenting is mastered by connecting with the fatherhood of Abba Father.

The fatherless need feel no disadvantage.

JULY 29

Pray intensely for what you don't have, but at the same time

exercise careful stewardship over what you do have.

Despising David did not make Michal barren; she was already barren.

It disqualified her from being healed in her womb.

———————————

Now as the ark of the LORD came into the City of David, Michal, Saul's daughter,

looked through a window and saw King David leaping and whirling before the LORD;

and she despised him in her heart...Therefore Michal the daughter of Saul

had no children to the day of her death.

2 Samuel 6:16, 23

Why did God release Paul and Silas from jail? Not simply to get them unstuck—they were about to be released the next morning anyways.

He did it for the drama. God loves to deliver His servants in a way that brings glory to His name and draws unbelievers to Himself.

Suddenly there was a great earthquake, so that the foundations of the prison were shaken; and immediately all the doors were opened and everyone's chains were loosed.

Acts 16:26

The guy whom God answered over and over (David) is the guy who prayed more than anyone else, "Hear me! Answer me!"

———————————————————

Hear me when I call, O God of my righteousness! You have relieved me in my distress; Have mercy on me, and hear my prayer.

Psalm 4:1

Are you in ravished, yearning, head-over-heels-crazy love for

the Inventor, Creator, and Overseer of hell?

_____

All things were made through Him, and without Him nothing was made that was made.

John 1:3

Now out of His mouth goes a sharp sword, that with it He should strike the nations.

And He Himself will rule them with a rod of iron. He Himself treads

the winepress of the fierceness and wrath of Almighty God.

Revelation 19:15

If you had to reduce the message of the Gospel to one word,

which word would you use?

My answer: Life! Jesus came to give us abundant life.

_____

"The thief does not come except to steal, and to kill, and to destroy. I have come

that they may have life, and that they may have it more abundantly."

John 10:10

To have a voice to an end-time generation suffering great calamities, you must be prepared by tasting it first.

In the day of great calamity, Job's friends were incapable of helping him process his sufferings. Why? They had never experienced that level of trauma themselves. When faced with it they were impotent to speak to it.

"For now you are nothing, you see terror and are afraid."

Job 6:21

One of the clear messages of the book of Job: Never assume that

blessing means God's favor, or that calamity means God's disapproval.

The cross is the greatest example of that truth. The lonely, tortured

figure on the tree was actually the most favored one on the hill.

The gifts of the Spirit are an itemized list of God-qualities.

God is all-wise, all-knowing, full of faith, healing, doing miracles, speaking oracles, all-discerning, and able to speak in every man's language.

For to one is given the word of wisdom through the Spirit, to another the word of knowledge through the same Spirit, to another faith by the same Spirit, to another gifts of healings by the same Spirit, to another the working of miracles, to another prophecy, to another discerning of spirits, to another different kinds of tongues, to another the interpretation of tongues.

1 Corinthians 12:8-10

Those who practice open homosexuality and immorality bring judgment on themselves because they do not hide their sin.

The openly gay lifestyles condoned by today's media is an utter shame to America. Refuse to be entertained by it.

"They declare their sin as Sodom; they do not hide it.

Woe to their soul! For they have brought evil upon themselves."

Isaiah 3:9

The Spirit says things to the churches. When you separate yourself from the churches, you won't hear what the Spirit is saying to them.

———————————————

"He who has an ear, let him hear what the Spirit says to the churches."

Revelation 3:13

What glorifies God is when we are delivered and give Him the credit for it.

Being in trouble doesn't glorify Him; it's our deliverance from trouble that glorifies Him. The saint who dies with unfulfilled promises is like a dud bomb that didn't explode.

"Call upon Me in the day of trouble; I will deliver you, and you shall glorify Me."

Psalm 50:15

Who is in charge of earthquakes and tsunamis, anyways?

According to Psalm 95:4, the tectonic plates

of the earth's crust are in God's hands.

_____

In His hand are the deep places of the earth.

Psalm 95:4

Christ's riven side is the fissure from which the geyser

of God's love erupts and flows to the world.

———————————————

The water was flowing from under the right side of the temple.

Ezekiel 47:1

One of the meanings of "declared" (Romans 1:4) is to mark out.

In resurrecting Christ, God was using His highlighter. "This is My Son."

Declared *to be the Son of God with power according to the Spirit of holiness,*

by the resurrection from the dead.

Romans 1:4

Likewise, when God resurrects you from your pit,

He crowns you with identity.

Resurrection is how God demonstrates you are His.

Have you ever wondered why salt was a required addition
to many of the sacrifices in Moses' covenant?

It prefigured the salty sweat of our Lord as He agonized
and labored at Calvary. The bull would have been killed
without having sweated.

But Jesus was not just killed, He was tormented
in an agonizing death. He sweated, both at Gethsemane and
on the cross, as He labored for our salvation.

"When you offer them...the priests shall throw salt on them,

and they will offer them up as a burnt offering to the LORD."

Ezekiel 43:24

When God raises up the one you crucified, you would do well

to get low and make peace with Him speedily.

———————————————————

"Jesus Christ of Nazareth, whom you crucified, whom God raised from the dead."

Acts 4:10

Approaching Calvary, Mary and Judas embody two attitudes toward money. Mary gives extravagantly, Judas hoards.

"For it might have been sold for more than three hundred denarii and given to the poor." And they criticized her sharply.

Mark 14:5

And when they heard it, they were glad, and promised to give him money. So he sought how he might conveniently betray Him.

Mark 14:11

Judas made money off the crucifixion.

When handling money, you are touching that which got Jesus crucified. Use it with trembling hands.

———————————————————

"What are you willing to give me if I deliver Him to you?"

And they counted out to him thirty pieces of silver.

Matthew 26:15

There is nothing—not even eternity itself—that will ever erase

from God's mind the slightest fraction of Calvary's horror.

With God a thousand years is as a day. To God, therefore,

Calvary happened just a couple days ago.

But, beloved, do not forget this one thing, that with the Lord one day is as

a thousand years, and a thousand years as one day.

2 Peter 3:8

The horrific torment of Calvary is as fresh in the mind

of God today as the moment it happened.

That's why the blood is so powerful when it touches your life!

Faith in the blood unlocks the infinite passions of an uncreated God.

_____

And behold...in the midst of the elders, stood a Lamb as though it had been slain.

Revelation 5:6

The cross compels us to ask, "What kind of a Father does something like this to His beloved Son?"

Viewed cynically, the cross appears to some as "cosmic child abuse." But the cross must be viewed in light of the resurrection which follows.

Resurrection not only raised up Christ, it also vindicated God as a good Father.

———————————

"I will be a Father to you."

2 Corinthians 6:18

The cross without resurrection *is* cosmic child abuse.

That's why crucifixion was never intended to be

the last chapter of your story.

At the Last Supper, John laid his head on the spot where,

hours later, the spear would pierce Jesus' side.

Your scars, Jesus, are my pillow.

Then, leaning back on Jesus' breast, he said to Him, "Lord, who is it?"

John 13:25

But one of the soldiers pierced His side with a spear,

and immediately blood and water came out.

John 19:34

A principle of resurrection: God raises and lifts you up

so that you might raise and lift Him up.

———————————————

"Glorify Your Son, that Your Son also may glorify You."

John 17:1

"I will set him on high, because he has known My name."

Psalm 91:14

AUGUST 24

The cross (His suffering, death, burial, resurrection, and ascension) is

the clearest revelation in all of Scripture of who God really is.

The cross forces everyone to choose sides.

You cannot remain neutral before it.

The cross surfaces everybody's loyalties.

Judas demonstrated loyalty only to himself. The chief priests remained loyal to their own standing in the nation. Pilate, when choosing between loyalty to Christ or to Caesar, chose Caesar without hesitation.

———————————————————

The Jews cried out, saying, "If you let this Man go, you are not Caesar's friend. Whoever makes himself a king speaks against Caesar." When Pilate therefore heard that saying, he brought Jesus out and sat down in the judgment seat.

John 19:12-13

Jesus demonstrated His loyalty to His Father even when utterly forsaken.

The cross is the ultimate symbol of loyalty.

"Father, if it is Your will, take this cup away from Me;

nevertheless not My will, but Yours, be done."

Luke 22:42

If all the fullness of God can dwell in Christ's physical, human body,

that means all of God's fullness can dwell in my body, too.

———————————————

For in Him dwells all the fullness of the Godhead bodily.

Colossians 2:9

The Gospel is most potent when miraculous healings accompany the preaching of the resurrection of Jesus.

One of the primary purposes of healing (raised up from sickness) is to confirm the reality of the resurrection (raised up from death).

So he, leaping up, stood and walked and entered the temple with them—walking, leaping, and praising God...[The priests were] greatly disturbed that they taught the people and preached in Jesus the resurrection from the dead.

Acts 3:8; 4:2

The church is reproached today for its impotence and compromise.

More disturbing, however, is how that reproach ultimately reflects upon God. He is profaned, patronized, mocked, and dismissed.

"Hallowed be Your name" must again be our first cry.

Why should the nations say, "Where is their God?"

Psalm 79:10

When God raises you up, the impact of your story will derive more from your cross season than your resurrection. For example, the power portion of Joseph's story comes not from his palace but his prison years.

While being crushed, you're building the part of your history that will put power into your testimony.

_____

But we preach Christ crucified, to the Jews a stumbling block and to the Greeks foolishness, but to those who are called, both Jews and Greeks, Christ the power of God and the wisdom of God.

1 Corinthians 1:23-24

The heart is a furnace.

Just as the walls of an oven keep a fire hot,

righteousness sustains love for Jesus.

Lawlessness dissipates it.

———————————————————

"And because lawlessness will abound, the love of many will grow cold."

Matthew 24:12

O blessed walls of righteousness that hem in my love!

The heart seeking fiery abandonment does not move the walls
out further, but draw them in even closer to make the flame hotter.

————————————————

If she is a wall, we will build upon her a battlement of silver.

Song of Solomon 8:9

Scripture likens men to trees.

There are two kinds of men. Some give knowledge
of good and evil, others impart life.

The tree of life was also in the midst of the garden,

and the tree of the knowledge of good and evil.

Genesis 2:9

Many who instruct in good and evil are sincere but unable to impart the power to choose righteousness. You find their thinking brilliant in illuminating evil, but there is no help in their logic to overcome the lust of the flesh.

In contrast, when you eat the fruit of someone who is a tree of life, you are empowered toward godliness.

The fruit of the righteous is a tree of life.

Proverbs 11:30

SEPTEMBER 5

The wilderness was supposed to test the Israelites, not God.

God's not on trial in your wilderness, you are. God's faithfulness has been proven over the centuries, you're the unproven one.

———————————

"In the day of trial in the wilderness...your fathers tested Me."

Psalm 95:8-9

At creation God consulted no advisors.

So I've decided to stop advising God on how to write my story.

With whom did He take counsel, and who instructed Him, and taught Him in the path of justice? Who taught Him knowledge, and showed Him the way of understanding?

Isaiah 40:14

SEPTEMBER 7

Promise forces you to judge God.

You must judge Him to be either good to His word or a liar.

———————————————

By faith Sarah herself also received strength to conceive seed, and she bore a child

when she was past the age, because she judged Him faithful who had promised.

Hebrews 11:11

The seraphim are worthy to look directly upon God,

but unworthy to look at the scroll.

What kind of scroll is this?

_____

And no one in heaven or on the earth or under the earth

was able to open the scroll, or to look at it.

Revelation 5:3

When Jesus created the human body, He began with a blank slate.

From a universe of options He chose the body you now inhabit.

Your body is superior to all the alternatives your Creator considered.

I will praise You, for I am fearfully and wonderfully made.

Psalm 139:14

Forming the human frame was pivotal because
Jesus was creating the body He would inhabit forever.

It had to be a body that could contain the fullness of God.

Your body contains everything needed to cooperate with God
and live in the Spirit.

For in Him dwells all the fullness of the Godhead bodily.

Colossians 2:9

The Spirit wars against your flesh but not against your body.

For the flesh lusts against the Spirit, and the Spirit against the flesh.

Galatians 5:17

The Spirit works in tandem with your body.

Your body is an asset, not a hindrance.

Do you know what you've got?

Mercy is not the sanctioning of compromise,

but the directing of the heart into holiness.

———————————————

Now may the Lord direct your hearts into the love of God and into the patience of Christ.

2 Thessalonians 3:5

Only do not use liberty as an opportunity for the flesh,

but through love serve one another.

Galatians 5:13

Mercy is the kindness of God to get you where you need to go,

in spite of yourself.

When the morning dawned, the angels urged Lot to hurry, saying, "Arise, take

your wife and your two daughters who are here, lest you be consumed in

the punishment of the city." And while he lingered, the men took hold of his hand,

his wife's hand, and the hands of his two daughters, the LORD being merciful

to him, and they brought him out and set him outside the city.

Genesis 19:15-16

Faithfulness is not the same as loyalty. Faithfulness has to do with servanthood, loyalty has to do with sonship.

He who was called "faithful and true" (Revelation 19:11) was both a faithful Servant and a true Son.

"'Well done, good and faithful servant.'"

Matthew 25:21

To Timothy, a true [loyal] son in the faith.

1 Timothy 1:2

We look at the Pharisees and call them legalistic; Jesus looked

and called them the opposite—lawless.

Although they had external regulations, they had no restraint on the

envy, pride, murder, lust, and greed of their inner souls.

———————————

"Woe to you, scribes and Pharisees, hypocrites! For you are like whitewashed tombs
which indeed appear beautiful outwardly, but inside are full of dead men's bones and all
uncleanness. Even so you also outwardly appear righteous to men, but inside you are
full of hypocrisy and lawlessness."

Matthew 23:27-28

There are some people groups that simply don't mix. Even a

shared religion, such as Islam, will not make them adhere.

This is one of the dynamics God uses to manage

the affairs of the nations.

_____

"As you saw iron mixed with ceramic clay, they will mingle with the seed of men;

but they will not adhere to one another, just as iron does not mix with clay."

Daniel 2:43

The reason Christians of all continents are bonded to one another

is because they have all been joined into one new nation.

———————————————

But you are a chosen generation, a royal priesthood, a holy nation.

1 Peter 2:9

The Lord's eyes that search the earth for a loyal heart are seven in number. What if all seven landed upon *you*?

"For the eyes of the LORD run to and fro throughout the whole earth,

to show Himself strong on behalf of those whose heart is loyal to Him."

2 Chronicles 16:9

And I looked, and behold...a Lamb as though it had been slain, having seven horns

and seven eyes, which are the seven Spirits of God sent out into all the earth.

Revelation 5:6

Imagine having such insight into the magnificence of God's decisions

that it causes you to erupt in praise multiple times every day!

Seven times a day I praise You, because of Your righteous judgments.

Psalm 119:164

The significance of the testimony determines the sphere of the eldership.

When God decides to widen your eldership,

He does so by enlarging your testimony.

For by it [faith] the elders obtained a good testimony.

Hebrews 11:2

Christ's sacrifice should awaken fear in our hearts because
we were redeemed at such an extravagant, bloody price!

We will give account for how we stewarded all the glorious benefits
of the precious, shed blood of Christ.

---

*Conduct yourselves throughout the time of your stay here in fear knowing that
you were not redeemed with corruptible things...but with the precious blood
of Christ, as of a lamb without blemish and without spot.*

1 Peter 1:17-19

SEPTEMBER 23

If God fears God, how much more should I?

Who, in the days of His flesh, when He had offered up prayers and supplications,

with vehement cries and tears to Him who was able to save Him from death,

and was heard because of His godly fear.

Hebrews 5:7

Jesus' confidence in His identity empowered Him to serve others in humility.

Humility and servanthood proceed from the security that comes from an established identity. Issues of insecurity, ignored or improperly faced, rob us of the freedom to serve others in humility.

Jesus, knowing that the Father had given all things into His hands, and that He had come from God and was going to God, rose from supper and laid aside His garments, took a towel and girded Himself.

John 13:3-4

SEPTEMBER 25

Saul was so pumped by his battle momentum that he didn't wait for God's counsel. The Saul test: Will you wait for divine orders even when the victory you desire is within your grasp?

The victory was not proof of divine favor, but was actually a test.

You can win the battle and fail the test.

Now it happened, while Saul talked to the priest, that the noise which was in the camp of the Philistines continued to increase; so Saul said to the priest, "Withdraw your hand." Then Saul and all the people who were with him assembled, and they went to the battle; and indeed every man's sword was against his neighbor, and there was very great confusion.

1 Samuel 14:19-20

Desperate in prison to understand his dreams, Joseph was driven
to go deep in dream interpretation.

The channels of understanding he dug in prison became the wellspring
that effected his release (see Genesis 41:9-14).

God induces His prisoners to press into the very thing
that will unlock their chains.

———————————

*Now there was a young Hebrew man with us there, a servant of the captain of the guard.
And we told him, and he interpreted our dreams for us; to each man he interpreted according to his own dream.*

Genesis 41:12

Those who eat food sacrificed to idols share in the altar
at which that food was sacrificed.

This principle applies to TV, movies, internet, etc. When
we are entertained by sins we ourselves would not commit,
we partake in what the sinners are offering.

———————————————

Are not those who eat of the sacrifices partakers [sharers] of the altar?
1 Corinthians 10:18

"Nevertheless I have a few things against you, because you allow that woman Jezebel,
who calls herself a prophetess, to teach and seduce My servants to commit sexual im-
morality and eat things sacrificed to idols."

Revelation 2:20

Boldness begets boldness.

When the believers saw how God honored the boldness of Peter and John before the Jewish council, it inspired them to ask for boldness.

Now, Lord, look on their threats, and grant to Your servants that with all boldness they may speak Your word, by stretching out Your hand to heal, and that signs and wonders may be done through the name of Your holy Servant Jesus.

Acts 4:29-30

One reason Jesus is so eager to lift you from your pit is because

He Himself knows what it feels like to need resurrecting.

For You will not leave my soul in Sheol.

Psalm 16:10

The two from Emmaus, in their conversation with Jesus,

did not utter any statements of overt unbelief.

They were just recounting facts and their own astonished responses.

But Jesus rebuked them for not swallowing whole

all the words of the prophets.

————————————————

"O foolish ones, and slow of heart to believe in all that the prophets have spoken!"

Luke 24:25

Satan wanted all the disciples, but asked especially for the foremost leader. Satan always targets the primary leaders first.

Those who ascend to places of leadership gain increased attention from both heaven and hell.

———————————

And the Lord said, "Simon, Simon! Indeed, Satan has asked for you, that he may sift you as wheat."

Luke 22:31

Lord, please do us a massive favor.

Make sin appear utterly ugly and exceedingly sinful to us.

That sin through the commandment might become exceedingly sinful.

Romans 7:13

Sometimes you have to reach a certain threshold of pain

before you're willing to make certain decisions.

———————————————————

They blasphemed the God of heaven because of their pains and their sores,

and did not repent of their deeds.

Revelation 16:11

True intimacy with Jesus impregnates you with divine life,

making you fruitful in the kingdom of God.

Therefore, my brethren, you also have become dead to the law through

the body of Christ, that you may be married to another—to Him who was raised

from the dead, that we should bear fruit to God.

Romans 7:4

When Jesus treads the winepress of the fierceness of God's wrath,
it will remind us of the day He cleansed the temple.

Those who objected to His temple cleansing cowered in silence
because of the sheer force of His personality.
We'll see the same forcefulness again.

Now out of His mouth goes a sharp sword, that with it He should strike the nations.

And He Himself will rule them with a rod of iron. He Himself treads

the winepress of the fierceness and wrath of Almighty God.

Revelation 19:15

Jesus is King of kings and Lord of lords. Today's kings are presidents and prime ministers. Today's lords are congressmen, senators, and judges.

At Jesus' return, all the renegade leaders of the earth will give account to the King. Leaders who are overly-eager to gain public office don't grasp the sobriety of giving account, eye to eye, with their Lord and King.

And He has on His robe and on His thigh a name written:

KING OF KINGS AND LORD OF LORDS.

Revelation 19:16

OCTOBER 7

Your spirit searches the Holy Spirit for two things—the *what* and the *when* of God's promises. The angels search into the very same things.

We have access to divine information that the angels do not have. They listen to apostolic preaching to learn more.

———————————————

Searching what, or what manner of time, the Spirit of Christ who was in them was indicating when He testified beforehand the sufferings of Christ and the glories that would follow. To them it was revealed that, not to themselves, but to us they were ministering the things which now have been reported to you through those who have preached the gospel to you by the Holy Spirit sent from heaven— things which angels desire to look into.

1 Peter 1:11-12

Divine perspective is empowering.

Earthly perspective calls affliction "devastating and debilitating."

Heavenly perspective sees it as "light and momentary."

———————————————————

For our light affliction, which is but for a moment, is working for us

a far more exceeding and eternal weight of glory.

2 Corinthians 4:17

There is a dimension of Jesus you'll never know until

you accompany Him to the harvest.

Come, my beloved, let us go forth to the field; let us lodge in the villages.

Let us get up early to the vineyards; let us see if the vine has budded,

whether the grape blossoms are open, and the pomegranates are in bloom.

There I will give you my love.

Song of Solomon 7:11-12

The greater the suffering, the greater the glory God can derive from it.

The cross is the best illustration of that truth.

God doesn't increase our giftings until we're equal to the task;

rather, He empties us until we realize our

absolute helplessness apart from Him.

———————————————————

"For without Me you can do nothing."

John 15:5

Weaning changes the appetite.

In weaning us, God withholds what we want in order
to change what it is that feeds us.

————————————————

Surely I have calmed and quieted my soul, like a weaned child with his mother;

like a weaned child is my soul within me.

Psalm 131:2

When you're in His presence for extended periods,

the molecular composition of your soul gets restructured.

Self-denial is the deliberate curtailing of healthy passions

and desires for the sake of pursuing Jesus harder.

––––––––––––––––––––

Then Jesus said to His disciples, "If anyone desires to come after Me,

let him deny himself, and take up his cross, and follow Me."

Matthew 16:24

God is not only an Initiator but also a Responder.

Move toward Him and He will definitely respond.

He is a rewarder of those who diligently seek Him.

Hebrews 11:6

Draw near to God and He will draw near to you.

James 4:8

The cross did not make the book of Job obsolete; rather,

it confirmed Job's relevance for New Covenant believers.

Indeed we count them blessed who endure. You have heard of the

perseverance of Job and seen the end intended by the Lord—

that the Lord is very compassionate and merciful.

James 5:11

Only one kind of righteousness gains access to the throne of God—pristine, immaculate, blazing, majestic, towering righteousness.

The only way to attain that kind of righteousness is by faith in Christ.

And be found in Him, not having my own righteousness, which is from the law,

but that which is through faith in Christ, the righteousness

which is from God by faith, that I may know Him.

Philippians 3:9-10

How to distinguish between righteousness and holiness:

Righteousness is what qualifies you to draw near to God.

Holiness is what happens to you when you get there.

Mercy was given to Paul because he was ignorant and unbelieving.

The things we suppose disqualify us from mercy are our very qualifiers.

I was formerly a blasphemer, a persecutor, and an insolent man;

but I obtained mercy because I did it ignorantly in unbelief.

1 Timothy 1:13

Although He was denuded, the cross could not strip Christ of the truth

that circled His waist and the barbed helmet of salvation on His brow.

Stand therefore, having girded your waist with truth...and take the helmet of salvation.

Ephesians 6:14, 17

OCTOBER 21

When the angel broke the Roman government's seal on Christ's tomb,

heaven was announcing its authority over every human government.

But national governments of the earth do not bow to Christ's sovereignty

willingly. History will end with a final showdown when

all the earth's kings unify to declare war against the Lamb.

"These will make war with the Lamb, and the Lamb will overcome them, for He is Lord of

lords and King of kings; and those who are with Him are called, chosen, and faithful."

Revelation 17:14

And I saw the beast, the kings of the earth, and their armies, gathered together to make

war against Him who sat on the horse and against His army.

Revelation 19:19

I say to my Father, "My hope is in You." He replies, "My hope is in you."

He means that Jesus (the Father's hope) is in me.

———————————————

God willed to make known what are the riches of...this mystery...

which is Christ in you, the hope of glory.

Colossians 1:27

To sustain Abraham's faith in the 25-year wait,

God repeatedly reiterated promises to him.

Expect the same.

I want to be like Abraham: A father to people, and a friend to God.

People looked at the young ruler's riches and called them assets;
Jesus look at them and called them "lack."

Assets in this life are liabilities in the kingdom unless
laid at the Master's feet.

Then Jesus, looking at him, loved him, and said to him, "One thing you lack:
Go your way, sell whatever you have and give to the poor, and you will have
treasure in heaven; and come, take up the cross, and follow Me."

Mark 10:21

In Mark 10:14 Jesus was greatly displeased. In Mark 10:41 the disciples were greatly displeased. See the great difference between the two.

Am I displeased with the things that displease Jesus?

But when Jesus saw it, He was greatly displeased *and said to them,*

"Let the little children come to Me, and do not forbid them;

for of such is the kingdom of God."

Mark 10:14

And when the ten heard it, they began to be greatly displeased *with James and John.*

Mark 10:41

It is highly significant to the kingdom which enemies of God
you choose to oppose.

Why? Because God beats down the foes against which you set your face.

"I will beat down his foes before his face, and plague those who hate him."

Psalm 89:23

"Mighty" in Isaiah 9:6 can be translated a champion,

hero, warrior, or mighty man.

Christ is our "Champion God."

And His name will be called Wonderful, Counselor, Mighty *God,*

Everlasting Father, Prince of Peace.

Isaiah 9:6

When the Lord sought a metaphor suitable to His anointing,

He chose oil not water.

Water evaporates quickly, but oil stays with you.

And John bore witness, saying, "I saw the Spirit descending from heaven

like a dove, and He remained upon Him."

John 1:32

The advice of ungodly people is not always evil, but it is always devoid of faith in divine intervention.

Only believers will give you counsel that demands an activation of faith.

Blessed is the man who walks not in the counsel of the ungodly.

Psalm 1:1

Here, in Psalm 1:2, is the key to day and night prayer and worship.

When you meditate in God's word, you can't help but pray over what
you read. You'll pray things like, "Oh God, give this truth to me!"
The way to mobilize saints to pray day and night, therefore,
is to motivate them to meditate in the word day and night.

In His law he meditates day and night.

Psalm 1:2

Give your loyalty only to leaders who preserve the three standards of Psalm 45:4—truth, humility, and righteousness.

Any leader who compromises one of these three areas (without repentance) hazards your loyalty.

_____

And in Your majesty ride prosperously because of truth, humility, and righteousness.

Psalm 45:4

Our hearts ache for believers for whom the Sunday morning sermon

is their only source of spiritual feeding.

Jesus didn't die for us to live off one meal a week. He died to give us

the abundant life of sitting daily at His feet and hearing His word.

The church is the body of Christ.

When a body is a business, isn't that a prostitute?*

———————————————————

The church, which is His body, the fullness of Him who fills all in all.

Ephesians 1:22-23

*Source: David Ryser

Tornadoes signal that seasons are changing.

May the Lord change your season with His tornado!

Then the LORD answered Job out of the whirlwind.

Job 38:1

If you're waiting on God for unfulfilled promises, you're in good company—Jesus also has promises from Abba for which He's waiting.

_____

The LORD said to my Lord, "Sit at My right hand,

till I make Your enemies Your footstool."

Psalm 110:1

The most militant thing you can do is draw near to God.

Revelation 15:3-4 contains the wonderful lyrics of a song co-written by Moses and the ultimate Songwriter—Jesus.

As they worked out the lyrics, doubtless Moses and Jesus rehearsed the song together. I bet the tune is unforgettable.

———————————————

They sing the song of Moses, the servant of God, and the song of the Lamb.

Revelation 15:3

Holiness is not merely the absence of sin; it's the presence of fire.

God rarely writes short stories.

The power of loyalty is in how it enables us to do more together than apart.

When Lucifer rebelled, heaven had a church split.

Which proves you can be the perfect pastor and still have a church split.

Fast from your little indulgences and pleasures, which keep your heart

close to your belly and crowd out kingdom perspective.

———————————————————

Whose end is destruction, whose god is their belly, and whose glory

is in their shame—who set their mind on earthly things.

Philippians 3:19

Anytime you change a fundamental truth of the personhood of Christ,

you have a new religion.

Your appearance before Christ on the Day of Judgment is going
to be a very personal encounter with Jesus.

When your eyes lock with His, the only important thing in the universe
at that moment will be the words that come out of His mouth.

For we must all appear before the judgment seat of Christ, that each one may receive

the things done in the body, according to what he has done, whether good or bad.

2 Corinthians 5:10

The inverse of this Scripture is equally true: What is highly esteemed in the sight of God is an abomination among men.

To what, then, are you devoted that is an abomination among men?

_____

"For what is highly esteemed among men is an abomination in the sight of God."

Luke 16:15

God put Joseph into prison, and God got Joseph out.

If you're in a Joseph prison, wait on God until He releases you.

"Shame" and "ashamed" are not the same. Shame is the temporary reproach you feel because your story is incomplete. Ashamed has to do with how the story ends.

You may feel shame while in process, but if you wait on God, you shall not be ashamed. He will not leave you unfinished but will clothe your life with completion.

———————————————

"For they shall not be ashamed who wait for Me."

Isaiah 49:23

I used to think you could tell someone's level of unresolved issues by the level of heat in their lives. "Huge flame, huge issues."

Then I saw Psalm 103:10, "He has not dealt with us according to our sins." He turns the fire up in your life, not based on your issues but based on your cry.

Example: The guy with all the issues (Saul) got none of the fire, while the guy with the heart after God (David) got all the fire.

When inspired by the outcome of someone's conduct,

follow that person's faith.

You can't follow someone else's conduct, but you can follow their faith.

Remember those who rule over you, who have spoken the word of God to you,

whose faith follow, considering the outcome of their conduct.

Hebrews 13:7

Never assume God's silence means no.

If God hasn't answered your prayer yet, here's what
you should take that to mean: He hasn't answered your prayer yet.
His silence is an invitation to wait on Him until He answers.

For all the promises of God in Him are Yes,

and in Him Amen, to the glory of God through us.

2 Corinthians 1:20

Here's why the journey to true spiritual greatness is so arduous:

God never makes the pathway to greater fruitfulness enviable.

Jesus affirmed that people went into the wilderness not to *hear* but to *see* John the Baptist. John was a burning and shining lamp, and people came from all over to watch him burn.

Leaders: People don't come to *listen* to you but to *watch* you. Get on fire for God and people will come watch you burn because everybody likes a bonfire.

As they departed, Jesus began to say to the multitudes concerning John:

"What did you go out into the wilderness to see?"

Matthew 11:7

I've heard it said, "Embrace the trial." But how can you embrace that from which God has promised to deliver you?

Hebrews 12:2 doesn't say Jesus embraced the cross, but that He *endured* the cross. Hebrews 11:13 doesn't say the saints embraced their trials, but that they embraced the *promises* of God's salvation.

Here's the rule for life: Endure the discipline, embrace the promise.

Looking unto Jesus...who for the joy that was set before Him endured the cross.

Hebrews 12:2

Not having received the promises, but having seen them afar off were assured of them, embraced them.

Hebrews 11:13

NOVEMBER 24

A branch does not labor to produce fruit;

it simply draws on the life in the vine.

———————————————

"I am the true vine...Every branch that bears fruit He prunes,

that it may bear more fruit."

John 15:1-2

The pruned often look at their quivering stub and think, "I'm ruined!"

But no matter how devastated you feel, cling to Christ. Get the life of God flowing into you, and you *will* be fruitful again. It's inexorable.

"I am the true vine...Every branch that bears fruit He prunes,

that it may bear more fruit."

John 15:1-2

The greatest battle ever fought was won by a Man

who just stood on the nail.

Therefore take up the whole armor of God, that you may be able to

withstand in the evil day, and having done all, to stand.

Ephesians 6:13

Don't just do something, stand there.

Therefore take up the whole armor of God, that you may be able to

withstand in the evil day, and having done all, to stand.

Ephesians 6:13

NOVEMBER 28

Use heartsickness to put down deep roots into God. Grow a root system.

Then, when the desire comes, your testimony will be a tree of life.

One thing about a tree: it feeds more than just you.

Hope deferred makes the heart sick, but when the desire comes, it is a tree of life.

Prov. 13:12

Christ's disciples were heartsick at His cross.

His resurrection turned a beating post into a tree of life.

Hope deferred makes the heart sick, but when the desire comes, it is a tree of life.

Prov. 13:12

To those with ears to hear, here's the Master Key to the Christian life.

Jesus gave it to us in four simple words, "Abide in My love" (John 15:9).

Devote the rest of your life to the inexhaustible depths
of that holy invitation.

Promise is a Person.

Fulfilled promises are always encounters with the Holy Spirit.

When you have your fingers wrapped around Promise,

you have hold of a piece of God.

He commanded them not to depart from Jerusalem,

but to wait for the Promise of the Father.

Acts 1:4

DECEMBER 2

In this passage, Paul contrasts the Holy Spirit with idols. Idols are mute

and unhearing, but the Holy Spirit is communicative by nature.

The spiritual gifts listed in 1 Corinthians 12 are expressions of a God

who hears and talks and communicates. Let Him talk through you.

Now concerning spiritual gifts, brethren, I do not want you to be ignorant:

You know that you were Gentiles, carried away to these dumb idols,

however you were led.

1 Corinthians 12:1-2

The spirit of wisdom is not the same thing as the spirit of revelation. Revelation is what we want; wisdom is how we get it.

My hunch: You're not going to get a revelation of Jesus while watching TV or playing video games.

Wisdom adopts a lifestyle that sets itself up for revelation.

That the God of our Lord Jesus Christ, the Father of glory, may give to you the spirit of wisdom and revelation in the knowledge of Him.

Ephesians 1:17

God placed the nation of Israel inside Egypt so they would grow.

For 430 years, Israel didn't suffer a single casualty to war.

Protected by the Egyptian army, they grew from a family of seventy

to a nation some three million strong.

God sends you into captivity to grow you.

When Israel finally emerged from Egypt, they were strong enough to *conquer*, *inhabit*, and *hold* their promised land.

Never waste a good prison sentence—get large enough to inhabit your promises.

He increased His people greatly, and made them stronger than their enemies.

Psalm 105:24

DECEMBER 6

Zacharias had but one prayer—a life-dominating prayer.
He wanted a child.

A life-dominating prayer is that one petition that dwarfs every
other request of your heart. When all the forces of your soul are
focused on gaining one thing, you are positioned for answered prayer.

———————————

*But the angel said to him, "Do not be afraid, Zacharias, for your prayer is heard; and
your wife Elizabeth will bear you a son, and you shall call his name John."*

Luke 1:13

Give yourself a longing test frequently.

Do you long for Jesus more than ever?

Do you still weep when in the word?

_____

As the deer pants for the water brooks, so pants my soul for You, O God.

Psalm 42:1

DECEMBER 8

I've discovered that many times when a Selah appears in a Psalm,

that verse will take your meditations to the cross of Christ.

In Psalm 143:6, for example, we see Christ with His hands spread

on the cross, crying out to His Father, "I thirst!"

Whenever you see a Selah, think cross.

_____

I spread out my hands to You; my soul longs for You like a thirsty land. Selah

Psalm 143:6

A manned cross is grossly detestable. So when it says
"the world has been crucified to me," it means that
the world has been made utterly abhorrent to me.

Reciprocally, when I have been crucified to the world,
the world looks at me and finds me altogether loathsome.

But God forbid that I should boast except in the cross of our Lord Jesus Christ,

by whom the world has been crucified to me, and I to the world.

Galatians 6:14

Leaders do not rule over the faith of the flock, nor is the faith of the flock dependent upon their relationship to their leaders. Each believer stands solely by faith in Jesus Christ.

Leaders are called to come alongside and labor on behalf of the faith and joy of believers.

Not that we have dominion over your faith, but are fellow workers for your joy; for by faith you stand.

2 Corinthians 1:24

The wilderness is the place where Jesus, in His mercy, dries up all the fountains that have been sustaining you.

DECEMBER 12

The cross, preached as an end in itself, loses its glory and purpose.

Devoid of resurrection, crucifixion is powerless.

On the other hand, when we only emphasize resurrection power

and don't value the role of crucifixion in our lives,

we actually strip resurrection of its brilliance.

For a story to attain biblical proportions, it must contain both a painful

crucifixion and a dramatic resurrection.

Mt. Carmel proved God is into showdowns.

_____

"Then you call on the name of your gods, and I will call on the name of the LORD;

and the God who answers by fire, He is God."

So all the people answered and said,

"It is well spoken."

1 Kings 18:24

God wants to write a story with your life.

So give Him some material to work with.

When you decide that the Lord will be your God, no matter what, you're giving God room to write your story. Take matters into your own hands and you pull out from under Him the basis upon which He would have written your great, last chapter.

Then Jacob made a vow, saying, "If God will be with me, and keep me in this way that I am going, and give me bread to eat and clothing to put on, so that I come back to my father's house in peace, then the LORD shall be my God."

Genesis 28:20-21

DECEMBER 16

If Jesus could have written the inscription over His cross,

I think it might have read, "'Now I come to You'" (John 17:13).

The cross was Jesus' pathway to the Father.

Similarly, our most direct path to the Father is by way of the cross.

Another lesson from the cross: People will no longer mock you

once you've expired.

I want to fall asleep every night with Jesus on my mind,

and then in the morning I want Him to be my first thought.

———————————————————

When I awake, I am still with You.

Psalm 139:18

When Jesus chose His disciples, He didn't travel far and wide to select the most stellar candidates in the earth. He simply chose from among the rank and file—ordinary men who lived nearby.

Don't assume that thriving ministries have somehow attracted unusually talented and gifted leaders. They're working with the same resource pool—ordinary folks like us.

And as He walked by the Sea of Galilee, He saw Simon and Andrew his brother casting a net into the sea; for they were fishermen. Then Jesus said to them, "Follow Me, and I will make you become fishers of men."

Mark 1:16-17

DECEMBER 20

How should one die? With the prayer of Stephen on your lips,

"Lord Jesus, receive my spirit" (Acts 7:59).

Complain right and God puts it in the Bible.

Complain wrong and He kills you.

Don't complain about God to others. If you have a complaint, take it directly to Him. Bring it to Him and He'll work it out with you—even if you have a bad attitude.

———————————————

I pour out my complaint before Him; I declare before Him my trouble.

Psalm 142:2

"He hears your complaints against the LORD. But what are we,

that you complain against us?"

Exodus 16:7

It is not a contradiction to pray for deliverance from

a calamity which is caused by God.

In fact, God intends for you to seek deliverance.

(For just one of many biblical examples, see Psalm 107:23-32.)

If the king lifts the scepter to Esther, we call her bold;

if he executes her, we call her presumptuous.

Fine line between boldness and presumption. Presumption is
boldness without commensurate relationship.

"Any man or woman who goes into the inner court to the king, who has not been called,

he has but one law: put all to death, except the one to whom the king

holds out the golden scepter, that he may live."

Esther 4:11

On the road to Damascus, God crafted for Paul a story
of uncommon impact. Paul told that story often in his travels—
because there's power on a good story.

Paul's Damascus road story had power to help people get a grip
on the kingdom who otherwise wouldn't have grasped it.
God is writing Damascus-caliber stories still today.

———————————————

"Now it happened, as I journeyed and came near Damascus at about noon, suddenly a
great light from heaven shone around me."

Acts 22:6

He is called "the Holy Spirit of promise" because

He's always promising things to God's people.

Listen closely and you'll hear Him whisper, "I am for you.

I will help you. I promise."

You were sealed with the Holy Spirit of promise.

Ephesians 1:13

You can't reach for what you don't see.

As you reach forward in obedience, God will lift the fog

and show you what you need to know about the journey ahead.

————————————————

But one thing I do, forgetting those things which are behind

and reaching forward to those things which are ahead.

Philippians 3:13

A disciple's job is to place stuff in Jesus' hands and then

watch what He does with it.

———————————————————

"Bring them here to me"...And He took the five loaves and the two fish, and looking up to heaven, He blessed and broke and gave the loaves to the disciples; and the disciples gave to the multitudes.

Matthew 14:18-19

Some people say you should never ask God why.

But I reckon if Jesus can ask why, I can too.

Actually, it's *essential* that we ask why because that's how

we discover divine purpose. God redeems every tragedy

surrendered to Him and infuses it with divine purpose.

———————————————

Jesus cried out with a loud voice...“My God, My God, why have You forsaken Me?”

Matthew 27:47

We can fall into the trap of relating to Jesus as a gas station—

a place to get filled for Christian service.

Once satisfied, we're on our way.

Things don't change when I talk to God;

things change when God talks to me.

When I talk, nothing happens. When God talks,

the universe comes into existence.

Effective prayer, therefore, often does more listening than speaking.

Then God said, "Let there be light"; and there was light.

Genesis 1:3

"Furthermore" is literally "even better."

God views resurrection as even better than crucifixion.

God *values* your crucifixion (because He knows all it will accomplish),

but He *prefers* your resurrection!

———————————————

Christ who died, and furthermore is also risen.

Romans 8:34

To order Bob's books or to inquire further into
his materials and ministry:

www.oasishouse.com

Oasis House
PO Box 522
Grandview, MO 64030-0522
816-767-8880

http://twitter.com/BOBSORGE
http://www.facebook.com/BobSorgeMinistry